Why Anne Died: the Nazi persecution of the Jews

You love hatred and want to measure the world against it.
You throw food to the beast in man,
That it may grow, the beast deep within you!
Let the beast in man devour man.

Erich Kastner from *Marschliedschen* (1932)

The hatred and prejudice that were to destroy Anne Frank and six million other European Jews, during the Second World War of 1939–45, began in the distorted mind of the German Nazi leader, Adolf Hitler. As a down-and-out, living in a doss-house in Vienna in the years just before the First World War, Hitler learned to hate Jews. This may have been caused by some sort of sexual humiliation by a Jewish girl, but anti-Semitism (hatred of Jews) was in any case widespread in Vienna at that time. In *Mein Kampf* (My Struggle, 1924), his autobiography and statement of policy, Hitler presented the reasons for his anti-Semitic feelings. He tries to appear reasonable and logical yet his hatred is based on no real evidence: it is a sick fantasy. By relentless and cunning propaganda, Hitler spread the hatred from his own mind to infect millions of others. One notorious Nazi school book saw Jews as the 'poisonous mushroom'. However, the phrase better describes Nazi anti-Semitism itself, growing in Germany and German-controlled areas in Europe with terrible speed. And hatred, as William Blake's famous poem, *A Poison Tree*, indicates, easily turns to violence and the lust to kill. The seed of hatred born in Hitler in Vienna when he first came to hate the Jews grew ultimately into the hideous Death Camps where Anne and millions of other Jews suffered and died.

The following extracts (pages 4–12) show the beginnings and the methods of Nazi anti-Semitism. They will help you to understand the background to Anne's Diary: why the family had to hide and why they died in Auschwitz and Belsen in 1945.

LITERATURE GUIDES

...DIARY OF ...NE FRANK

...opher Martin

Series editors:
John Griffin
Theresa Sullivan

Introduction

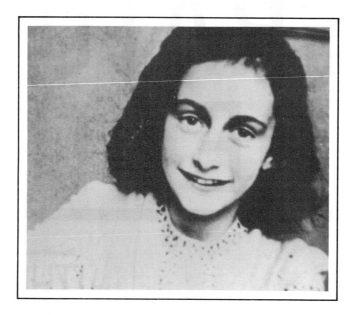

Her voice was preserved out of the millions that were
silenced, this voice no louder than a child's whisper. It
tells how those millions lived, spoke, ate, and slept,
and it has outlived the shouts of the murderers and
has soared above the voices of time.

Ernst Schnabel in his conclusion to
The Footsteps of Anne Frank

Anne Frank wrote one of the most remarkable of all published diaries. Anne was a
German Jewish girl whose family fled the Nazi persecution of Jews in Germany in the
1930s, settling in what they hoped was the safety of Amsterdam, Holland. When the
Nazis invaded Holland in 1940, the terror returned and the Franks went into hiding in a
Secret Annexe, hidden rooms at the back of Otto Frank's business premises in
Amsterdam.

Anne's Diary records the fears and strains of this life in hiding. As a record of war or
of the Nazi persecution of Jews in Europe, the Diary is an outstanding document. Yet it
is a personal record, too, a tender and moving picture of Anne's adolescence. Her
experience was unique yet we may all see something of ourselves in her delicately
noted thoughts and feelings. Anne's ultimate fate – death in Belsen concentration camp –
gives the Diary an extra dimension of poignancy: we share Anne's life in the Annexe so
closely that we almost relive the experience with her. Then Anne's voice is abruptly and
brutally silenced.

It is important you read *The Diary of Anne Frank* before you begin the work in this
book. Then, as you go through the historical background provided here (both written
and pictorial), the Diary and the strange life it records should be easier to understand.
There are many suggestions for GCSE coursework (written and oral) based on the Diary:
you will be asked to write letters, poems, diary entries and play scenes; to react to
photographs and paintings of the time; and to discuss the various issues raised in the
Diary and in the historical evidence presented here.

Extracts from *Mein Kampf*

Once, when passing through the Inner City, I suddenly encountered a phenomenon in a long caftan and wearing black sidelocks. My first thought was: Is this a Jew? They certainly did not have this appearance in Linz. I watched the man stealthily and cautiously; but the longer I gazed at that strange countenance and examined it feature by feature, the more the question shaped itself in my brain: Is this a German?

I could no longer doubt that here there was not a question of Germans who happened to be of a different religion but rather that there was question of an entirely different people. For as soon as I began to investigate the matter and observe the Jews, then Vienna appeared to me in a different light. Wherever I now went I saw Jews and the more I saw of them the more strikingly and clearly they stood out as a different people from the other citizens. Especially the Inner City and the district northwards from the Danube Canal swarmed with a people who even in outer appearance bore no similarity to the Germans.

Cleanliness, whether moral or of another kind, had its own peculiar meaning for these people. That they were water-shy was obvious on looking at them and, unfortunately, very often also when not looking at them at all. The odour of those people in caftans often used to make me feel ill. Beyond that there were the unkempt clothes and the ignoble exterior.

All these details were certainly not attractive; but the revolting feature was that beneath their unclean exterior one suddenly perceived the moral mildew of the chosen race.

What soon gave me cause for very serious consideration were the activities of the Jews in certain branches of life, into the mystery of which I penetrated little by little. Was there any shady undertaking, any form of foulness, especially in cultural life, in which at least one Jew did not participate? On putting the probing knife carefully to that kind of abscess one immediately discovered, like a maggot in a putrescent body, a little Jew who was often blinded by the sudden light.

In my eyes the charge against Judaism became a grave one the moment I discovered the Jewish activities in the Press, in art, in literature and the theatre. All unctuous protests were now more or less futile. One needed only to look at the posters announcing the hideous productions of the cinema and theatre, and study the names of the authors who were highly lauded there, in order to become permanently adamant on Jewish questions. Here was a pestilence, a moral pestilence, with which the public was being infected. It was worse than the Black Plague of long ago. And in what mighty doses this poison was manufactured and distributed!

The fact that nine-tenths of all the smutty literature, artistic tripe and theatrical banalities had to be charged to the account of people who formed scarcely one per cent of the nation – that fact could not be gainsaid. It was there and had to be admitted. Then I began to examine my favourite 'World Press' with that fact before my mind.

The deeper my soundings went, the lesser grew my respect for that Press which I formerly admired. Its style became still more repellent and I was forced to reject its ideas as entirely shallow and superficial. To claim that in the presentation of facts and views its attitude was impartial seemed to me to contain more falsehood than truth. The writers were – Jews.

I saw the Liberal policy of that Press in another light. Its dignified tone in replying to the attacks of its adversaries and its dead silence in other cases now became clear to me as part of a cunning and despicable way of deceiving the readers. Its brilliant theatrical criticisms always praised the Jewish authors and its adverse criticism was reserved exclusively for the Germans.

I now realized that the Jews were the leaders of Social Democracy. In face of that revelation the scales fell from my eyes. My long inner struggle was at an end.

Making an effort to overcome my natural reluctance, I tried to read articles of this nature published in the Marxist* Press; but in doing so my aversion increased all the more. And then I set about learning something of the people who wrote and published this mischievous stuff. From the publisher downwards, all of them were Jews. I recalled to mind the names of the public leaders of Marxism, and then I realized that most of them belonged to the Chosen Race – the Social Democratic representatives in the Imperial Cabinet as well as the secretaries of the Trades Unions and the street agitators. Everywhere the same sinister picture presented itself.

One fact became quite evident to me. It was that this alien race held in its hand the leadership of that Social Democratic Party with whose minor representatives I had been disputing for months past. I was happy at last to know for certain that the Jew is not a German.

Thus I finally discovered who were the evil spirits leading our people astray.

Should the Jew, with the aid of his Marxist creed, triumph over the people of this world, his crown will be the funeral wreath of mankind, and this planet will once again follow its orbit through ether, without any human life on its surface, as it did millions of years ago.

And so I believe to-day that my conduct is in accordance with the will of the Almighty Creator. In standing guard against the Jew I am defending the handiwork of the Lord.

* Marxists: communists (particular opponents of Hitler)

▷ What were Hitler's various reasons for hating the Jews?
Discuss which words and phrases, and comparisons, express Hitler's hatred most strongly.
What evidence does he give to support his claims?
How would you answer his arguments?

(*Above*) The madness and fanaticism of Hitler spread to millions of his followers: spectacular show of strength at a Nazi rally.
(*Below*) The hypnotic power of Hitler's speeches.

Street violence

As soon as Hitler became Chancellor of Germany in 1933, prejudice against Jews turned to open violence. A horrified British newspaper correspondent reported several incidents in Berlin. 'Brown Shirts' were uniformed Nazi thugs.

The worst excesses here in Berlin occurred on March 9th, most of the victims living in the Grenadierstrasse. Many Jews were beaten by Brown Shirts until the blood streamed down their heads and faces and their backs and shoulders were bruised. Many fainted and were left lying on the streets, and were picked up by friends or passers-by and taken to hospital. A man and his wife walking together were both beaten and robbed.

The Brown Shirts worked in gangs of five to thirty, the whole gang often assaulting one person. Many had the brassards worn by Nazis enrolled in the auxiliary police. Mr. —— was beaten bloody and unconscious and several hundred marks (his name and the precise sum are known to your correspondent) were taken from him.

Twelve uniformed men broke into the house of Mr. ——, stole several thousand marks and beat him, his wife, and his son until all three were bruised and bleeding (name, address, and precise sum also known).

On the evening of the 15th three Jews were arrested by Brown Shirts in the Cafe New York and taken in a car (the number of which is in the possession of your correspondent) to the S.A. Lokal in the Wallnertheaterstrasse, where they were robbed of several hundred marks (precise sum also known), beaten bloody with rubber truncheons, and then turned out on the streets in a semi-conscious state.

On the same day four Jews were taken to a Nazi S.A. Lokal in the Schillingstrasse, robbed of 400 marks and beaten bloody until they fainted.

Hundreds of Jews have been beaten, but not one dare say so publicly or dare complain without the risk of another beating.

Manchester Guardian, 27 March 1933

▷ Discuss what motives, apart from anti-Semitism, are seen here. What is so sinister about the Nazis wearing brassards? Why does the reporter mention precise sums, names, etc. in brackets?

Jews and Aryans

A popular Nazi fantasy claimed that there was a pure 'Aryan' German race, that was threatened with corruption and decay by contact with Jews. Look at these paintings of 'ideal' Aryan Germans. What qualities do the artists admire in male and female?

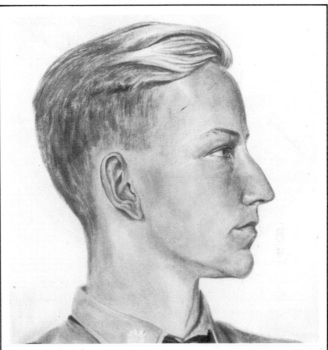

Ideal Aryan faces painted by two race obsessed artists: Oskar Just and Wolfgang Willrach.

▷ Look at these Nazi propaganda pictures of Jews.
What physical, mental and social features of the Jew do
the propagandists seek to put across to their audience?

Anti-Jewish propaganda: a beermat with the slogan: He who buys
from Jews is a traitor to his people.

Poster for the Film 'The Eternal Jew'. The Jew seen as cruel
exploiter and the inspiration behind Communism.

Burning the books

In May 1933, the Nazis launched a new campaign: to burn 'Un-German books'. Read the newspaper article opposite, published in *The Times* in 1933.

▷ Why do you think this gesture was so important to the Nazis? Why was it so sinister and symbolic?

Neo-Fascist groups in recent times have been anxious to prove that Anne Frank's Diary was a forgery. How is that claim connected to the burning of the books?

Un-German books destroyed
A Berlin bonfire

About 20,000 'Marxist', pacifist, Jewish, or other 'un-German' books, 'collected' by the Nazi-led students of Berlin University during recent days from public libraries and private owners, were burnt tonight in the Opera Place in Berlin in the presence of Dr. Goebbels, the Minister for Propaganda.

The burning began at 11.30. A dozen students each carrying a book, were shepherded in turn by the Nazi organizer to the microphone, where each recited an appropriate couplet, ending with the words, 'I consign to the flames the writer Emil Ludwig' or whoever the writer was. Then Dr. Goebbels stepped into the glare of the searchlights and the bonfire, and declaimed against the 'filth' of the Jewish 'asphalt literature'.

In place of the literature destroyed a list of desirable books has been compiled and recommended. . . . The list includes books extolling and explaining the principles of National Socialism, books on the theme of 'Nordic Racial Purity' and books romanticising war and explaining the virtues of a martial training.

The Times, 11 May 1933

Der Stürmer

This Nazi weekly newspaper was the chief of anti-Semitic propaganda. This typically crude and savage front page, with its headline 'Jewish murder plot' and its slogan 'The Jews are our misfortune', uses the obscene 'blood libel', revived by the Nazis: the idea that Jews used the blood of murdered Christian children in making their Passover bread. A rhyme goes with the picture:

For thousands of years the Yid has spilled
Man's blood his sacred rites to build.
Upon our necks the fiend still sits.
It's up to you to see he flits.

In August 1935, the editor addressed his readers:

> *Nuremberg A, 26th August, 1935.*
>
> DEAR STÜRMER-READER!
>
> The Jewish plague has eaten its way deep into the German people. Serious are the crimes that still to-day the Jew commits against the German people.
>
> Thanks to the mighty struggle that *The Stürmer* for 13 years has tirelessly waged against Jewish criminality, hundreds of thousands have successfully been rescued from the talons of the Jew. But many millions must be made conscious of the Jewish plague.
>
> In order finally to root out criminal Jewish people, a mighty campaign of enlightenment must be carried through, embracing the whole nation.
>
> My dear *Stürmer*-reader! We know you are a true Jew-hater. You have realised in time the danger that threatens us from the Jew, and therefore a great and holy task awaits you.
>
> Spread wide *The Stürmer* and see that it reaches the remotest German family.
>
> Fight with us in this colossal fight against the devil's people of Jewry.
>
> Every nation that has trusted and believed in the Jew has been infected with his virus and utterly ruined.
>
> That is why we are appealing to you.
>
> *Who fights alongside The Stürmer,*
> *fights for his people!*
>
> HEIL HITLER!

▷ What crude comparisons does the writer use to whip up anger against the Jewish people?

The Nazis and education

It was the Nazi education policy that finally persuaded Mr Frank to take his family out of Germany in 1933. Jewish children were expelled from German schools: no Jewish teachers were to be employed; schools and universities were to teach Nazi propaganda – even *Der Stürmer* was to be studied in class.

The effects of such school teaching can be seen in a pupil's essay sent in to *Der Stürmer* (page 11).

District Leader Streicher has told us so much about the Jews that we really hate them awfully. We were set a composition in school on 'The Jews are our Misfortune.' I should like you to publish mine:

"Unfortunately, many people still say nowadays: 'The Jews, too, are God's creatures. That's why you must hold them in respect.' But we say: 'Vermin are also creatures, yet we destroy them. The Jew is a mongrel. He has the traits of Aryan, Asiatics, Negroes and Mongols. In any mongrel the bad part is always uppermost. The only good thing the Jews have is their white skin.' The South Sea Islanders have a proverb: 'The White man comes from God and the Black man comes from God. But the mongrel is from the Devil.' Jesus once told them: 'Your father is not God, but the Devil.' The Jews hold to a wicked law. This is the Talmud. The Jews consider us as animals and treat us accordingly. They take our money and goods from us by cunning.

The Jew Gruneberg in Gelsenkirchen sold us stinking meat. This he is allowed to do by his own Law. The Jews have begun revolts and provoked wars. They have brought Russia into misery. In Germany they gave money to the Communist Party and paid all the rogues to murder. We stood at the brink of the grave. Then came Adolf Hitler. Now the Jews are abroad spreading atrocity lies against us. But we don't listen to them and we follow our Leader. We don't buy from Jews. Every penny we give them kills one of our people.

HEIL HITLER!

Erna Listing.

Der Stürmer also published attractive-looking children's books to reinforce the message of hatred. *Trust no fox and no Jew* appeared in 1936. Its colourful, ugly pictures were supported by a text of cruel rhymes:

This is the Jew as you can see,
The biggest rogue in Germany.
The face he thinks so very fair
Is ugly beyond all compare.

'Twas merry at our school to-day,
Because the Jews must go away.
The big ones and the small ones,
The short ones and the tall ones.
No sobs avail, no tears can help,
Out with the Jew dog and his whelp.

Jewish children and a teacher expelled from school: 'discipline and order' can now be taught.

In 1937, a prose book, *The Poisonous Mushroom*, appeared. Its hideous illustrations show Jews as corrupters of the young: the pure, Aryan girl faces the Jewish doctor: 'behind his glasses gleam the eyes of a 'criminal'; the Jewish sex-fiend gives out sweets to children. The healthy German boy shows his classmates that the Jewish nose is like the number 6.

▷ What do you find most disturbing about this propaganda aimed at the young? Why do you think the Nazis were so concerned to influence schoolchildren?

Use the information in this section

▷ Imagine that you are a Jew who stayed in Germany in the 1930s. Write to Mr Frank describing some of the worst features of the Nazis' persecutions of Jews. Use the pictures and written extracts given here as the basis for your writing.

▷ Anne asked:

Who has inflicted this upon us? Who has made us Jews different to all other people? Who has allowed us to suffer so terribly? (Letter 131, 11/4/44)*

Use the material given in this section to describe to Anne some of the Nazi prejudices against the Jews. Try to explain some of the reasons behind their mad fantasies.

* Throughout this book, Anne Frank's Diary letters will be referred to by letter number (as in the Longman Imprint Edition of *The Diary of Anne Frank*) and by date (this letter was written on the 11th of April, 1944).

Anne's background: some facts

1889	Father, Otto Frank, born into wealthy Jewish banking family, who had lived in Frankfurt-on-Main, Germany, since the seventeenth century. The city was known for its tolerance of Jews, declared to have equal status to other Germans in the early nineteenth century. After High School, Otto studied briefly at Heidelberg University.
1908	Worked in department store in New York.
1909–14	Worked for engineering company in Dusseldorf.
1914–18	Served in German Army. Promoted to Lieutenant. Decorated for courage.
1918	Onwards. Worked in father's bank and in business.
1925	Marriage of Otto and Edith (born 1900, daughter of wealthy manufacturer from Aachen).
1926	Margot born.
1929	June 12 – Anne (Annelies Marie) born.
1933	Hitler's seizure of power. Otto invited by Swiss brother-in-law to set up a branch of the German firm, Travies and Co., in Amsterdam, Holland. The firm sold various household and food products. This move allowed Otto to save his family from Hitler's persecution.
1934	Edith and her daughters moved to Amsterdam, after a year in Aachen with her family. Her mother ('Granny' – 'Grandma' was on father's side) moved with them. The family settled in the new suburb of Merwedeplein in south Amsterdam. Anne and Margot attended the good and progressive Montessori school, which they both loved.
1940	Otto's firm moved to 263 Prinsengracht, where the Secret Annexe was to be sited. Two ex-Austrians, Victor Kraler and Miep Gies, had worked with him for several years; now he was joined by Herman Van Daan (a Dutch-born Jew, who had lived in Germany, and had married a German), a spice expert, and Jo Koophuis, another Dutchman. Elli Vossen was the company typist.

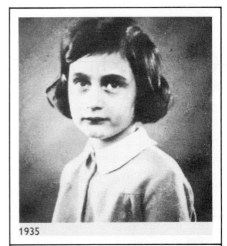
1935

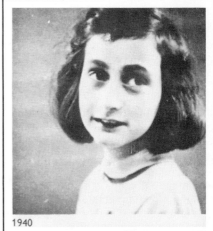
1940

1942

Anne growing up.

▷ In Letter 3 (20/6/42), Anne gives her own sketch of the family history. Write a summary of the family history, using the facts in this letter.

The Diary

Going into hiding

After the Nazi occupation of Holland in May 1940, the Franks were again trapped. Over the next two years 'the noose around the Jewish neck tightened' as the Franks' friend Miep Gies expressed it. The network of restrictions of Jewish activity is noted in Anne's Letter 3 (20/6/42). Dutch Nazi papers tried to turn Holland against the Jews. Some of the stories were fantastic: Jews had bitten the necks of German soldiers and sucked their blood like vampires! The *razia* (the Dutch word for 'round-up') became familiar in Amsterdam streets as leading Jews were captured and sent to death in concentration camps. In this climate of growing terror, Otto Frank, like thousands of other Jews, began to prepare a hiding place for his family.

In January 1940, his Travies Company had moved into larger premises in a seventeenth-century building on the Prinsengracht canal in the old centre of Amsterdam. At the back of the building was a set of unused rooms. The largest of these became, briefly, a laboratory, where another German-Jewish exile, a chemist hired by Mr Frank, sometimes made experimental new products for the company.

In December 1941, Otto Frank began to prepare his disappearance, moving stores and furniture into the rooms. He took his partner Koophuis and his assistant Miep Gies into his confidence: they became his secret helpers. The family of his other business associate, Van Daan, was to share the hiding place. The move was planned for 16 July 1942.

However, on Sunday, 5 July, a postcard from the authorities called up sixteen year old Margot Frank for forced labour in Germany. Although he was not entirely ready, Otto Frank moved swiftly to take his family into the Secret Annexe.

Re-read Letters 10, 11, 12, 13 (8/7/42–11/7/42) that give Anne's version of the move into hiding. Then read Miep Gies's account of the same events:

It was the first Sunday in July, a warm summer night. Henk and I, Mrs Samson and the others had eaten our evening meal and were all doing our various activities. For me Sunday evening meant doing small things to get ready for a new work week.

These days anything unusual was immediately upsetting, and when there came an insistent ringing of our bell the tension in the apartment rose up at the sound. Our eyes darted from one to the other. Quickly Henk went to the door and I followed him. There stood Mr Van Daan in quite an agitated condition. Henk and I spoke quietly to him, not wanting to upset Mrs Samson and her family.

'Come right away,' Van Daan entreated in a hushed but urgent voice. 'Margot Frank has received a postcard ordering her to appear for forced labour shipment in Germany. She's been ordered to bring a suitcase with winter things. The Franks have decided to go immediately into hiding. Can you come right now to take a few things that they'll need? Their preparations aren't complete, you see.'

'We will come,' Henk told him. We put on our raincoats. Carrying bags and packages would be too dangerous; we could hide much under our baggy old raincoats. It might appear odd to be wearing raincoats on a warm, dry summer night but it was better than carrying bags full of possessions.

Henk made some explanation to Mrs Samson so as not to alarm her and the others, and we left with Mr Van Daan. When Mr Frank had confided in me about the hiding plan, I had that very night told Henk about our conversation. Without discussion, Henk had affirmed his unconditional assistance to the Franks and agreed that the plan was a sound one. But neither of us had expected the Franks to go into hiding so soon. Walking quickly, but not hurrying in order not to attract attention, we went towards the Merwedeplein. On the way Van Daan told us that Mr Frank had just told his girls about the hiding plan but not about where the hiding-place was.

'You can imagine,' he explained, 'they're in a state of great confusion. There's so much to do and so little time and their damned lodger seems to be hanging about making it all quite difficult.'

Walking to the Franks', I suddenly felt a great sense of urgency for my friends. Conscripting a sixteen-year-old girl for forced labour was a new abomination the Germans were inflicting on the Jews. Yes, I thought, the sooner our friends got safely out of sight the better. And how many more young girls like Margot had they conscripted? Girls with no father like Mr Frank and no hiding plan? Girls who must be horribly frightened tonight. With these thoughts I had to force myself not to run the rest of the way to the Merwedeplein.

When we arrived at the Franks' flat few words were exchanged. I could feel their urgency, an undercurrent of near panic. But I could see that much needed to be organized and prepared. It was all too terrible. Mrs Frank handed us piles of what felt like children's clothes and shoes.

I was in such a state myself that I didn't look. I just took and took as much as I could, hiding the bunches of things the best way I could under my coat, in my pockets, under Henk's coat, in his pockets. The plan was that I'd bring these things to the hiding-place at some later date when our friends were safely inside.

With our coats bursting Henk and I made our way back to our rooms and quickly unloaded what we had under our coats. We put it under our bed. Then, our coats empty again, we hurried back to the Merwedeplein to get another load.

Because of the Franks' lodger the atmosphere at the Franks' flat was muted and disguised. Everyone was making an effort to seem normal, not to run, not to raise a voice. More things were handed to us. Mrs Frank bundled and sorted quickly, and gave to us as we again took and took. Her hair was escaping from her tight bun into her eyes. Anne came in bringing too many things; Mrs Frank told her to take them back. Anne's eyes were like saucers, a mixture of excitement and terrible fright.

Henk and I took as much as we could and quickly left.

Early the next day, Monday, I woke to the sound of rain.

Before seven-thirty, as we had arranged the night before, I had ridden my bicycle to the Merwedeplein. No sooner had I reached the front stoop than the door of the Franks' apartment opened and Margot emerged. Her bike was standing outside. Mr and Mrs Frank were inside and Anne, wide-eyed in a nightgown, hung back inside the doorway.

I could tell that Margot was wearing layers of clothing. Mr and Mrs Frank looked at me. Their eyes pierced mine.

I made an effort to be assuring. 'Don't worry. The rain is very heavy. Even the Green Police won't want to go out in it. The rain will provide a shelter.'

'Go,' Mr Frank instructed us, taking a look up and down the square. 'Anne and Edith and I will come later in the morning. Go now.'

Without a backward glance Margot and I pushed our bicycles on to the street. Quickly we pedalled away from the Merwedeplein, going north at the first turning. We pedalled evenly, not too fast, in order to appear like two everyday working girls on their way to work on a Monday morning.

Not one Green Policeman was out in the downpour. I took the big crowded streets from Merwedeplein to Waalstraat, then to the left to Noorden Amstellaan to Ferdinand Bolstraat, Vijzelstraat to Rokin Dam Square, Raadhuisstraat, finally turning on to the

Prinsengracht, never so glad before to see our cobbled street and murky canal.

All the way we had not said one word. We both knew that from the moment we'd mounted our bicycles we'd become criminals. There we were, a Christian and a Jew without the yellow star riding on an illegal bicycle. And at a time when the Jew was ordered to report for a forced labour brigade about to leave for parts unknown in Hitler's Germany. Margot's face showed no intimation. She betrayed nothing of what she was feeling inside. Suddenly we'd become two allies against the might of the German beast among us.

Not a soul was about on the Prinsengracht. We carried our bicycles into the storeroom. I unlocked the door to the office with my key. I shut the door against the rain. We were soaked through to the skin. I could see that Margot was suddenly on the verge of crumbling.

I took her arm and led her past Mr Frank's office and up the stairway to the landing that led to the hiding-place. It was approaching the time that the others would be coming to work. I was now afraid that someone would come but I kept silent.

Margot was now like someone stunned, in shock. I could feel her shock now that we were inside. As she opened the door I gripped her arm to give her courage. Still we said nothing. She disappeared behind the door, and I took my place in the front office.

My heart, too, was thumping. I sat at my desk wondering how I could get my mind on to my work. The pouring summer rain had been our shelter. Now one was safe inside the hiding-place. Three more had to be protected by the rain.

Mr Koophuis arrived at work and took Margot's bicycle somewhere I didn't know. Soon after he left I could hear the ware-houseman arriving, stamping the water off his shoes.

'So we walked in the pouring rain, Daddy, Mummy, and I . . . .' A last taste of freedom before Anne goes into hiding: A still from the 1986 BBC TV production of the Diary.

Late in the morning I heard Mr and Mrs Frank and Anne coming through the front office door. I had been waiting for that moment and quickly joined them and hurried them along past Mr Kraler's office up that stairway to the door of the hiding-place. All three of them were quite wet. They were carrying a few things and each had yellow stars sewn on to their clothes. I opened the door for them and shut it when they had vanished inside.

In the afternoon when no one was around and all was quiet I went upstairs to that door myself and disappeared into the hiding-place, closing the door tightly behind me.

Entering the rooms for the first time I was surprised by what I saw. In total disorder were sacks and boxes and furnishings, piles of things. I could not imagine how all these things had been brought up to the hiding-place. I had not once noticed anything being brought in. Perhaps it had been brought at night, or on Sundays when the office was closed.

On the first floor there were two quite small rooms. One was rectangular with a window, and the other long and thin, also with a window. The rooms were wood-panelled, the wood painted a dark green, the wallpaper old and yellowish and peeling in places. The windows were covered by thick white curtains. There was a toilet in a large room and a dressing area off to the side.

Up a steep old wooden flight of steps was a larger room with sink and stove and cabinets. Here, too, the windows were covered with thick white curtains. Off this large room was another rickety stairway to an attic and storage area. The steps to the attic cut through a garret-type tiny room, again filled with piles and sacks of things.

Mrs Frank and Margot were lost people, drained of blood, in conditions of complete lethargy. They appeared as though they couldn't move. Anne and her father were making efforts to make some order out of the multitude of objects, pushing, carrying, clearing. I asked Mrs Frank, 'What can I do?'

She shook her head. I suggested, 'Let me bring some food?'

She acquiesced. 'A few things only, Miep, maybe some bread, a little butter, maybe milk?'

The situation was so upsetting. I wanted to leave the family alone together. I couldn't begin to imagine what they must be feeling to have walked away from everything they owned in the world – their home, a lifetime of gathered possessions, Anne's little cat, Moortje. Keepsakes from the past. And friends.

They had simply closed the door of their lives and had vanished from Amsterdam. Mrs Frank's face said it all. Quickly I left them.

Miep Gies: *Anne Frank Remembered*

▷ Using material from Anne's and Miep's accounts, write an imaginative description of the move into the Annexe from the viewpoint of Margot. Start with the arrival of the call-up postcard and end at nightfall on Monday.

▷ Make a play scene out of the events of the Sunday from 3 p.m. until midnight. Remember to include the awkward lodger.

▷ Write a dialogue between Mr and Mrs Frank after the move. He explains; she regrets.

The Secret Annexe

Study the picture of 263 Prinsengracht and the drawing of the Annexe. Then re-read Anne's Letters 11 (9/7/42), 13 (11/7/42) and 15 (21/8/42) describing the Annexe.

▷ Imagine you walk through the Annexe, entering by the hidden door. Which scenes from the Diary come to your mind as you walk from room to room?

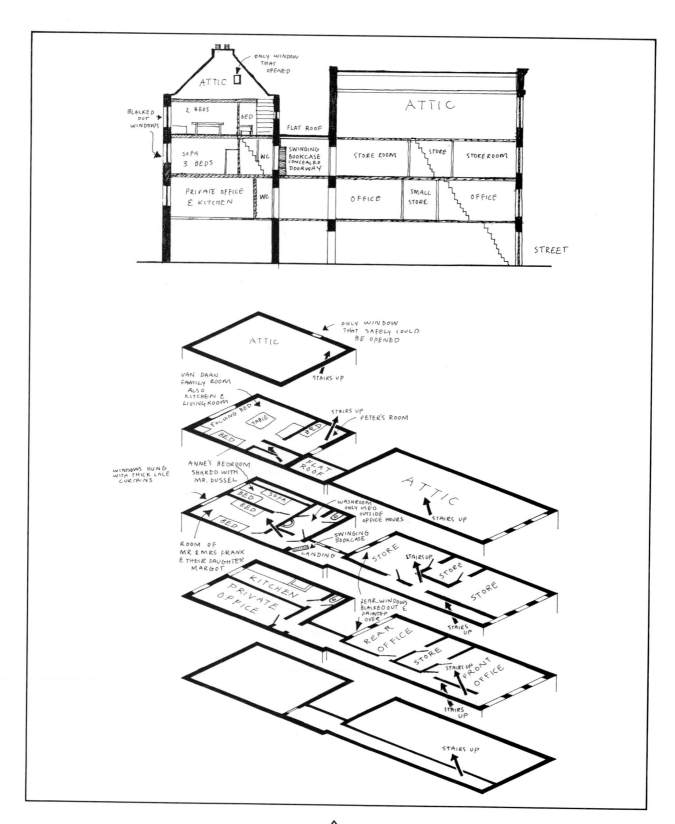

Anne's chestnut tree

Secret Annexe

The Warehouse

Westertoren Church

The Prinsengracht Canal

The spice warehouse and Secret Annexe from the air.

Miep Gies, the brave helper of the families, volunteered to sleep a night in the Annexe. Here is her description of the experience.

▷ Imagine you have been invited to spend a day and a night in the Annexe with the families. Write down your experiences and feelings. Use the descriptions by Anne and Miep to give you ideas and details.

Anne directed us towards the bedroom she shared with Margot. Henk and I had been allotted her room at Anne's insistence. Anne and Margot were going for the night into the room with their parents. Anne pulled me to her bed, neatly made up, and told me she wanted me to put my things there. Amused, I told her that I'd be honoured, and put my night things on her bed, Henk's on Margot's bed.

Shortly it was time for the radio broadcasts, and the entire group trooped down to Frank's office below to pull chairs up and gather around the Philips radio on the table. The whole room bristled with excitement when the near and yet so far voice of Radio Orange came through the radio. 'Here is Radio Orange. All things went well today. The English . . .', and on it went, filling us with hope and with information, our only real connection to the still-free outside world.

When it was time to sit down to eat, Henk and I were given seats of honour, as we had been on our anniversary dinner. All nine of us squeezed in around the table.

This time Mrs Frank and Margot had supervised the cooking. The food was tasty and filling.

With the blackout frames up and the electric light on, along with the heat from the cooking, the room became toasty warm, cosy. We sat long over coffee and dessert, talking, our friends devouring the novelty of our presence. They seemed to be insatiable for our company.

As I sat I became aware of what it meant to be imprisoned in these small rooms. As this feeling registered I felt a taste of the helpless fear that these people were filled with, day and night. Yes, for all of us it was wartime, but Henk and I had the freedom to come and go as we pleased, to stay in or go out. These people were in a prison, a prison with locks inside the doors.

Reluctantly we said good-night, remembering that Mr and Mrs Van Daan could not go to bed until we'd gone. Henk and I and the Frank family trooped down the stairway to the floor below. Here we said a second round of good-nights, and Henk and I got ready for bed in our little room, surrounded by Anne's movie-star faces on the wall.

I climbed into Anne's hard little bed which was very toasty with blanket upon blanket, so many blankets that I couldn't imagine how Anne could ever be taken with a chill. The room was cool otherwise, and as I settled in as cosily as I could, I could hear every sound being made in the old rooms; Mr Van Daan coughing, the squeak of springs, the sound of a slipper dropping beside a bed, the toilet flushing, Mouschi landing on his padded feet somewhere above me.

The Westertoren clock struck at fifteen-minute intervals. I'd never heard it so loud: it echoed and reverberated through the rooms. The church was right across the back gardens from the 'Annexe'. In the office down below the building blocked the sound. During the day by the time I heard the ringing in my front office the sound had been muted and cushioned by the entire building. It was soothing and distant.

All through the night I heard each ringing of the Westertoren clock. I never slept, I couldn't close my eyes. I heard the sound of a rainstorm begin, the wind come up. The quietness of the place was overwhelming. The fright of these people who were locked up here was so thick I could feel it pressing down on me. It was like a thread of terror pulled taut. It was so terrible it never let me close my eyes.

For the first time I knew what it was like to be a Jew in hiding.

Miep Gies: *Anne Frank Remembered*

The Diary as a record of history

Although Anne was hidden away from the daily world, the radio kept her in contact with events, and her own powerful sympathetic imagination allowed her to understand the sufferings of her fellow Jews in Europe:

In the evening when it is dark, I often see rows of good, innocent people accompanied by crying children, walking on and on, bullied and knocked about until they almost drop. No one is spared – each and all join in the march of death. (Letter 33, 9/11/42).

The dangers and sufferings of the war were all about her: air raids were a constant nightmare (what would happen if the Annexe were hit and caught fire?), and her glimpses of the poverty and deprivation outside (seen through the front windows of the building) were echoed by increasing poverty – poor clothing and inadequate diet – inside the Annexe itself. The atmosphere of fear is the most powerful aspect of Nazi-dominated Europe that Anne describes.

▷ As if you are Anne, write an essay about the sufferings of Jews in Europe based on what you have heard. Use these letters to prepare notes for this piece of writing: 3 (20/6/42), 6 (24/6/42), 10 (8/7/42), 24 (9/10/42), 33 (19/11/42); 38 (12/12/42), 49 (27/3/43), 81 (27/11/43), 131 (11/4/44), the end of the letter, 155 (22/5/44), and 156 (25/5/44).

▷ Study this famous photograph of Jewish families being rounded up in the Warsaw ghetto in Poland. Write an imaginative story about one or more of the people in the picture.

Graphic picture of fear as Jews from the Warsaw ghetto are rounded up by Nazi stormtroopers.

▷ Look at this protest painting, *The prayer of the killed*, by the Polish artist, Bronislaw Linke. The striped garment is a Jewish prayer shawl. What does the artist want to tell us about Europe and the Jews? Discuss whether you think the picture is effective or merely strange.

▷ What does the Diary tell us about the sufferings of civilians in Holland during the Second World War? Use these letters in preparing notes for a piece of writing on this theme: 24 (9/10/42), 38 (12/12/42), 40 (13/1/43), 44 (10/3/43), 52 (27/4/43), 54 (18/5/43), 60 (19/7/43), 62 (26/7/43), 97 (28/1/44), 98 (3/2/44), 115 (14/3/44), 122 (23/3/44), 125 (29/3/44), 128 (3/4/44), 145 (6/5/44).

Anne: the self portrait

'Little bundle of contradictions': that is how her family described Anne. She herself felt strongly the idea that she had a dual personality, that there were two Annes, the 'pure' being that she wanted to be, and the 'frolicksome little goat' that others judged her to be. This feeling is not uncommon in adolescents as they struggle to form an adult personality.

▷ Discuss the many aspects of Anne that the Diary offers us. Find places in the text that show her contradictory features, that she was:

deeply concerned for others
introspective (quiet, looking into herself)
deeply loving and caring
strong
profound in her view of the war and the
   fate of the Jews
open and honest
mature and shrewd in her insights into
   other people
idealistic

selfish
lively, comic, full of high spirits
unpleasant to others
weak and frightened
concerned with petty details
practical
secretive
naive (simple and childish)

Using some of the above points that you have discussed, write a character study of Anne herself.

'The prayer of the killed' by Bronislaw Linke.

▷ What are some of the changes you notice in Anne during the twenty-six months of the Diary?

▷ Write about some of the things and experiences that Anne missed about life outside the Annexe: Letters 1–10 (14/6/42–8/7/42), 61 (23/7/43), 84 (24/12/43), 90 (6/1/44), 91 (7/1/44), 99 (12/2/44), 105 (23/2/44), 113 (7/3/44), 132 (14/4/44), 147 (8/5/44), 164 (15/6/44).

▷ Describe some of the pleasures and interests that Anne found for herself in her strange Annexe life: Letters 17 (21/9/42), 35 (28/11/42), 38 (12/12/42), 45 (12/3/43), 68 (10/8/43), 71 (23/8/43), 92 (12/1/44), 96 (27/1/44), 105 (23/2/44), 113 (7/3/44), 129 (4/4/44), 130 (6/4/44), 137 (19/4/44), 140 (27/4/44), 150 (11/5/44).

Write a poem or an imaginative essay about Anne's joy in nature, even in her restricted circumstances.

▷ Compose Diary entries for two or more of the days where Anne left gaps.

▷ Write about Anne's difficulties in enduring life in the Annexe: Letters 13 (11/7/42), 17 (21/9/42), 19 (27/9/42), 20 (28/9/42), 28 (7/11/42), 35 (28/11/42), 39 (22/12/42), 41 (30/1/43), 44 (10/3/43), 45 (12/3/43), 52 (27/4/43), 53 (1/5/43), 57 (11/7/43), 58 (13/7/43), 62 (26/7/43), 63 (29/7/43), 73 (16/9/43), 75 (17/10/43), 76 (29/10/43), 78 (8/11/43), 97 (28/1/44), 123 (27/3/44), 128 (3/4/44), 156 (25/5/44).

▷ Discuss Anne's deeper thoughts about life:
her feelings about prejudice against Jews (Letter 131, 11/4/44);
her arguments against war (Letter 143, 3/5/44);
her thoughts about work (Letter 169, 6/7/44);
her ideals about people (Letter 171, 15/7/44).

One of the last photos of Anne, taken at school in 1941.

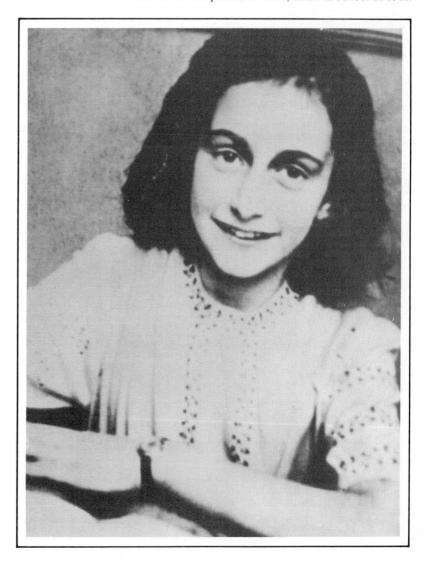

Anne and her parents

The Diary is a tribute to the warmth and devotion of Jewish family life. The fact that Anne kept the Diary in her father's briefcase and was assured of absolute privacy reveals the care and respect shown to her by her parents.

Yet the Diary is also an intimate record of those stresses between parent and child inevitable in adolescence. The claustrophobia of the Annexe heightened those feelings.

▷ Writing as if you were Anne, describe her changing feelings about her parents. Here are some quotations from the Diary to start you thinking.

I have darling parents. (Letter 3, 20/6/42)

Mummy sometimes treats me like a baby, which I can't bear. (Letter 15, 21/8/42)

Just had a big bust up with Mummy for the umpteenth time. (Letter 19, 27/9/42)

I told Daddy that I'm much more fond of him than Mummy. (Letter 23, 3/10/42)

Mummy, Margot and I are as thick as thieves again. (Letter 25, 16/10/42)

I adore Daddy. He is the one I look up to. I don't love anyone in the world but him. (Letter 28,7/11/42)

I'd like to stamp my feet, scream, give Mummy a good shaking. (Letter 41, 30/1/43)

Lately Mummy and I have been getting on better together, but we still *never* confide in each other. (Letter 43, 27/2/43)

'How can you be so unkind, how can you bring yourself to cause your mother such sorrow?' (Letter 51, 2/4/43)

I miss having a real mother who understands me. (Letter 84, 24/12/43)

Now it is suddenly clear to me what she lacks. Daddy avoids all arguments about Mummy. (Letter 89, 5/1/44)

Daddy doesn't want me to go upstairs so much in the evenings. (Letter 142, 2/5/44)

Daddy is not pleased with me . . . He doesn't want any 'necking'. (Letter 144, 5/5/44)

'Anne, you have done us a great injustice.' (Letter 146, 7/5/44)

I concealed from Daddy everything that perturbed me. I was aware of the fact that I was pushing him away from me. (Letter 171, 15/7/44)

▷ Re-read the episode of the letter to father: Letters 142 (2/5/44), 144 (5/5/44), 145 (6/5/44), 146 (7/5/44). Write about the difficulties of the incident from the viewpoints of:
Anne   Mr Frank   Mrs Frank   Margot

or Imagine a conversation between Mr and Mrs Frank about Anne's relationship with Peter.

Anne and Peter

The love story of Anne and Peter, carried on in such strange circumstances, is one of the important threads in the Diary story, coming to dominate it during 1944. It gave Anne hope and interest in her claustrophobic life, but it also caused her problems with her family and his, and, in the end, had its disappointments.

It is important not to confuse Peter Van Daan with Peter Wessel, Anne's childhood sweetheart and 'chosen one', glimpsed in Letter 7, (30/6/42), and the subject of the romantic dream in Letter 90 (6/1/44).

▷ Write an account of the relationship of Anne and Peter. You may attempt the whole story, or choose certain episodes within it. You may write from the outside, that is, from your point of view, or from the viewpoint of either Peter or Anne.

You may use details from the essay, 'My first interview' opposite (from *Tales from the Secret Annexe*, Anne's non-Diary writings), which gives many extra points about Peter and his room.

You may find all, or some, of the quotations from the Diary (page 26) useful in building an outline for your writing. The last points are particularly important to balance the picture.

My first interview

I wanted to write about somebody, and as I already had described most of the other people in the house, I thought of Peter. The boy always keeps himself in the background and, like Margot, never causes dissension.

If, towards evening, you knock on the door of his room and hear him call a soft 'Come in!' you may be sure that, on opening the door, you'll find him looking at you through two of the steps of the ladder to the attic and saying, 'So!' in a gentle, inviting tone.

His little room is – what is it really? I think it is a passage to the attic, very narrow, very draughty, but – he has turned it into a room. When he sits at the left of the ladder, there's surely no more than a yard's space between him and the wall. There stand his little table, laden, like ours, with books (a few steps of the ladder also hold some of his possessions) and a chair.

On the other side of the ladder, his bike hangs from the ceiling. Useless at present, it is carefully wrapped in brown paper, but a small chain, dangling from one of the pedals, is still visible.This corner is completed by a lamp with an ultra-modern shade, made from a piece of card-board covered with strips of paper.

I am still standing in the open door, and now I look in the other direction. Against the wall – that is, opposite Peter and behind the table – stands an old divan, covered with blue flowered stuff: the bedclothes have been hidden (but not quite successfully) behind it. Above the daybed hangs a lamp, the mate of the other one, and similarly decorated. A bit further on, there is a small bookcase filled, from top to bottom, with paper-covered books that could belong only to a boy. A hand-mirror is fastened to the wall beside it. Probably because the owner didn't know where else to put it, a small tool chest stands on the floor. (I know from experience that anything in the way of a hammer, a knife, or a screwdriver one may need, can be found in its depths.)

Near the bookcase, a shelf, covered with paper that once was white, was originally meant for such things as milk bottles, but has been converted into an annexe of the library; it all but groans under the weight of books. The milk bottles have become neighbours of the tool chest, on the floor.

Two of the walls are covered with green jute, and the other two are generously plastered with pictures of more or less beautiful movie stars and advertising posters. Grease and scorch spots should cause no surprise, for it is to be expected that, with so much stuff in a small space, something or other is bound to get dirty in a year and a half. The beamed ceiling, also, is no longer in good condition and, since there are leaks in the roof and Peter's room is in the attic, he has spread some sheets of cardboard to catch the drip. Innumerable water spots and rings show that this protection is far from adequate.

There's a sharp difference in Peter's appearance on weekdays and Sundays. Weekdays he wears cover-alls, from which he rarely separates himself, as he objects to having the things washed too often. I can't imagine the reason for this attitude, except that he fears his favourite piece of apparel might wear out that way. At any rate, it just has been laundered, and its colour – blue – is once more recognizable. Round his neck Peter wears a blue scarf, which apparently is just as dear to him as the cover-alls. A heavy, brown leather belt and white woollen socks complete his weekday attire. But on Sundays Peter's clothing may be said to undergo a rebirth. Then he wears a handsome suit, a fine pair of shoes, a shirt, a necktie – everything that belongs to a young man's nice wardrobe.

So much for Peter's appearance. As for the man himself, I have changed my opinion radically of late. I used to think him dumb and slow, but nowadays he is neither the one nor the other. Everybody agrees that he has grown into a fine young fellow. I know in my heart that he is honest and generous. He has always been modest and helpful, and I think that he is much more sensitive than people give him credit for. He has one preference that I shall never forget – the cats. Nothing is too much trouble where Mouschi or Moffi are concerned, and I do believe that those two sense that there isn't much love in his life and try to make up for it.

He's not afraid – on the contrary – and not as smart-alecky as other boys of his age. He isn't stupid, either, and has a remarkably good memory. That he is handsome I needn't say, for everyone who sees him knows that. His hair is wonderful – a wealth of fine brown curls. He has grey-blue eyes, and – describing faces has always been my weak point. After the war I'll paste his photo, together with those of the other people who were in hiding with us, in this book by way of illustration. That will save me the trouble of describing them.

▷ What features of Peter does Anne find attractive on this visit? What does she find interesting or amusing about his room and his possessions?

Peter, the Van Daans' son, arrived . . . He is not yet 16, a rather soft, shy, gawky youth; can't expect much from his company. (Letter 14, 14/8/42)

I still don't like Peter any better, he is so boring; he flops lazily in his bed half the time, does a bit of carpentry and then goes back for another snooze. What a fool. (Letter 15, 21/8/42)

Now and then Peter comes out of his shell and can be quite funny. We have one thing in common . . . We both love dressing up. He appeared in one of Mrs Van Daan's very narrow dresses and I put on his suit . . . (Letter 22, 1/10/42)

Margot and Peter aren't a bit what you would call 'young', they are both so staid and quiet. (Letter 42, 5/2/43)

Young Mr Van Daan is very quiet and doesn't draw much attention to himself. (Letter 67, 9/8/43)

My longing to talk to someone became so intense that somehow or other I took it into my head to choose Peter . . .
It gave me a queer feeling each time I looked into his deep blue eyes. (Letter 90, 6/1/44)

I made a special effort not to look at him too much, because whenever I did, he kept on looking too, and then – yes, then – it gave me a lovely feeling inside . . . (Letter 100, 13/2/44)

I have a strong feeling that Peter and I are really not so different as we would appear to be. (Letter 106, 27/2/44)

Peter Wessel and Peter Van Daan have grown into one Peter, who is beloved and good. (Letter 107, 28/2/44)

I wish we dared to tell each other much more. (Letter 110, 3/3/44)

A little shadow had fallen on my happiness. I've thought for a long time that Margot liked Peter quite a lot too. (Letter 120, 20/3/44)

Remember yesterday's date for it is a very important day in my life . . . (Letter 134, 16/4/44)

Is there anything more beautiful in the world than to sit before an open window and enjoy nature, to listen to the birds singing, feel the sun on cheek and have a darling boy in your arms? (Letter 137, 19/4/44)

Is it right that I should have yielded so soon, that I am so ardent, just as ardent and eager as Peter himself? (Letter 141, 28/4/44)

I asked Peter whether he thought I ought to tell Daddy a bit about us . . . (Letter 142, 2/5/44)

He's a darling, but I soon closed up my inner self from him. (Letter 153, 19/5/44)

Peter is good and he's a darling, but still there's no denying that there's a lot about him that disappoints me . . . (Letter 163, 14/6/44)

Here are two versions of the same event: the arrest of the hiders in the Secret Annexe by the Gestapo, the German secret police.

The first is from the play version of the Diary by Albert and Frances Hackett. The second is from *The Footsteps of Anne Frank* (1958) by Ernst Schnabel, a German who devotedly traced the story of Anne before and after the two years in the Secret Annexe. He interviewed dozens of eye-witnesses who filled in missing details of Anne's short life. Read the two versions.

The play scene

It is an afternoon a few weeks later . . . Everyone but Margot is in the main room. There is a sense of great tension.
Both Mrs Frank and Mr Van Daan are nervously pacing back and forth. Dussel is standing at the window, looking down fixedly at the street below. Peter is at the centre table, trying to do his lessons. Anne sits opposite him, writing in her diary. Mrs Van Daan is seated on the couch, her eyes on Mr Frank as he sits reading.
The sound of a telephone ringing comes from the office below. They all are rigid, listening tensely. Mr Dussel rushes down to Mr Frank.

Dussel There it goes again, the telephone! Mr Frank, do you hear?

Mr Frank [*quietly*] Yes. I hear.

Dussel [*pleading, insistent*] But this is the third time, Mr Frank! The third time in quick succession! It's a signal! I tell you it's Miep, trying to get us! For some reason she can't come to us and she's trying to warn us of something!

Mr Frank Please. Please.

Mr Van Daan [*to Dussel*] You're wasting your breath.

Dussel Something has happened, Mr Frank. For three days now Miep hasn't been to see us! And today not a man has come to work. There hasn't been a sound in the building!

Mrs Frank Perhaps it's Sunday. We may have lost track of the days.

Mr Van Daan [*to Anne*] You with the diary there. What day is it?

Dussel [*going to Mrs Frank*] I don't lose track of the days! I know exactly what day it is! It's Friday, the fourth of August. Friday, and not a man at work. [*He rushes back to Mr Frank, pleading with him, almost in tears.*] I tell you Mr Kraler's dead. That's the only explanation. He's dead and they've closed down the building, and Miep's trying to tell us!

Mr Frank She'd never telephone us.

Dussel [*frantic*] Mr Frank, answer that! I beg you, answer it!

Mr Frank No.

Mr Van Daan Just pick it up and listen. You don't have to speak. Just listen and see if it's Miep.

Dussel	[*speaking at the same time*] For God's sake . . . I ask you.
Mr Frank	No. I've told you, no. I'll do nothing that might let anyone know we're in the building.
Peter	Mr Frank's right.
Mr Van Daan	There's no need to tell us what side you're on.
Mr Frank	If we wait patiently, quietly, I believe that help will come.

There is silence for a minute as they all listen to the telephone ringing.

Dussel	I'm going down. [*He rushes down the steps. Mr Frank tries ineffectually to hold him. Dussel runs to the lower door, unbolting it. The telephone stops ringing. Dussel bolts the door and comes slowly back up the steps.*] Too late. [*Mr Frank goes to Margot in Anne's bedroom.*]
Mr Van Daan	So we just wait here until we die.
Mrs Van Daan	[*hysterically*] I can't stand it! I'll kill myself! I'll kill myself!
Mr Van Daan	For God's sake, stop it!

In the distance, a German military band is heard playing a Viennese waltz.

Mrs Van Daan	I think you'd be glad if I did! I think you want me to die!
Mr Van Daan	Whose fault is it we're here? [*Mrs Van Daan starts for her room. He follows, talking at her.*] We could've been safe somewhere . . . in America or Switzerland. But no! No! You wouldn't leave when I wanted to. You couldn't leave your things. You couldn't leave your precious furniture.
Mrs Van Daan	Don't touch me!

She hurries up the stairs, followed by Mr Van Daan. Peter, unable to bear it, goes to his room. Anne looks after him, deeply concerned. Dussel returns to his post at the window. Mr Frank comes back into the main room and takes a book, trying to read. Mrs Frank sits near the sink, starting to peel some potatoes. Anne quietly goes to Peter's room, closing the door after her. Peter is lying face down on the cot. Anne leans over him, holding him in her arms, trying to bring him out of his despair.

Anne	Look, Peter, the sky. [*She looks up through the skylight.*] What a lovely, lovely day! Aren't the clouds beautiful? You know what I do when it seems as if I couldn't stand being cooped up for one more minute? I *think* myself out. I think myself on a walk in the park where I used to go with Pim. Where the jonquils and the crocus and the violets grow down the slopes. You know the most wonderful part about thinking yourself out? You can have it any way you like. You can have roses and violets and chrysanthemums all blooming at the same time . . . It's funny . . . I used to take it all for granted . . . and now I've gone crazy about everything to do with nature. Haven't you?
Peter	I've just gone crazy. I think if something doesn't happen soon . . . if we don't get out of here . . . I can't stand much more of it!
Anne	[*softly*] I wish you had a religion, Peter.
Peter	No, thanks! Not me!
Anne	Oh, I don't mean you have to be Orthodox . . . or believe in heaven and hell and purgatory and things . . . I just mean some religion . . . it doesn't matter what. Just to believe in something! When I think of all that's out there . . . the trees . . . and flowers . . . and seagulls . . . when I think of the dearness of you, Peter . . . and the goodness of

the people we know . . . Mr Kraler, Miep, Dirk, the vegetable man, all risking their lives for us every day . . . When I think of these good things, I'm not afraid any more . . . I find myself, and God, and I . . .

Peter interrupts, getting up and walking away.

Peter That's fine! But when I begin to think, I get mad! Look at us, hiding out for two years. Not able to move! Caught here like . . . waiting for them to come and get us . . . and all for what?

Anne We're not the only people that've had to suffer. There've always been people that've had to . . . sometimes one race . . . sometimes another . . . and yet . . .

Peter That doesn't make me feel any better!

Anne [*going to him*] I know it's terrible, trying to have any faith . . . when people are doing such horrible . . . But you know what I sometimes think? I think the world may be going through a phase, the way I was with Mother. It'll pass, maybe not for hundreds of years, but some day . . . I still believe, in spite of everything, that people are really good at heart.

Peter I want to see something now . . . Not a thousand years from now!

He goes over, sitting down again on the cot.

Anne But, Peter, if you'd only look at it as part of a great pattern . . . that we're just a little minute in the life . . . [*She breaks off.*] Listen to us, going at each other like a couple of stupid grown-ups! Look at the sky now. Isn't it lovely? [*She holds out her hand to him. Peter takes it and rises, standing with her at the window looking out, his arm around her.*] Some day, when we're outside again, I'm going to . . .

She breaks off as she hears the sound of a car, its brakes squealing as it comes to a sudden stop. The people in the other rooms also become aware of the sound. They listen tensely. Another car roars up to a screeching stop. Anne and Peter come from Peter's room. Mr and Mrs Van Daan creep down the stairs. Dussel comes out from his room. Everyone is listening, hardly breathing. A doorbell clangs again

and again in the building below. Mr Frank starts quietly down the steps to the door. Dussel and Peter follow him. The others stand rigid, waiting, terrified. In a few seconds Dussel comes stumbling back up the steps. He shakes off Peter's help and goes to his room. Mr Frank bolts the door below, and comes slowly back up the steps. Their eyes are all on him as he stands there for a minute. They realize that what they feared has happened. Mrs Van Daan starts to whimper. Mr Van Daan puts her gently in a chair, and then hurries off up the stairs to their room to collect their things. Peter goes to comfort his mother. There is a sound of violent pounding on a door below.

Mr Frank [*quietly*] For the past two years we have lived in fear. Now we can live in hope.

The pounding below becomes more insistent. There are muffled sounds of voices, shouting commands.

Men's voices Auf machen! Da drinnen! Auf machen! Schnell! Schnell! Schnell! etc., etc.

The street door below is forced open. We hear the heavy tread of footsteps coming up. Mr Frank gets two school bags from the shelves, and gives one to Anne and the other to Margot. He goes to get a bag for Mrs Frank. The sound of feet coming up grows louder. Peter comes to Anne, kissing her good-bye, then he goes to his room to collect his things. The buzzer of their door starts to ring. Mr Frank brings Mrs Frank a bag. They stand together, waiting. We hear the thud of gun butts on the door, trying to break it down.
Anne stands, holding her school bag, looking over at her father and mother with a soft, reassuring smile. She is no longer a child, but a woman with courage to meet whatever lies ahead.
The lights dim out. The curtain falls on the scene. We hear a mighty crash as the door is shattered. After a second Anne's voice is heard.

Anne's voice And so it seems our stay here is over. They are waiting for us now. They've allowed us five minutes to get our things. We can each take a bag and whatever it will hold of clothing. Nothing else. So, dear Diary, that means I must leave you behind. Goodbye for a while. P.S. Please, please, Miep, or Mr Kraler, or anyone else. If you should find this diary, will you please keep it safe for me, because some day I hope . . .

Her voice stops abruptly. There is silence.

▷ Discuss the following:

1 Which words in the first few stage directions help to create tension?
2 Why is the ringing of the telephone dramatic?
3 Why does the silence of the building worry the hiders?
4 How does the distant German music add to the effect of the scene?
5 What happens to the Van Daan family when danger threatens?

6 What differences of attitude and character in Anne and Peter are seen here?
7 Which famous words of Anne are built into her speech?
8 What is the point of Mr Frank's comment at the moment of arrest?
9 What qualities of the soldiers are given prominence in the arrest?
10 What is the point of Anne's last speech?

From *The Footsteps of Anne Frank*

What happened in the house on the Prinsengracht on that fourth of August, 1944, was far less dramatic than it is now depicted on the stage. In reality the cars did not approach with howling sirens, did not stop with screaming brakes in front of the house. The bell was not rung. No rifle butt rapped against the door till it reverberated as it now reverberates in the theatre every night somewhere in the world. The truth was, at first no one heard a sound. They were practised, skilful, and quiet in such cases.

Mr Koophuis says:
'It was a Friday, and a fine August day. The sun was shining; we were working in the big office, Miep, Elli, and myself, and in the warehouse below us the spice mills were rumbling. When the sun was shining the trees along the canal and the water itself would often cast flecks of light on the ceiling and walls of the office, ripples of light that flickered and danced. It was an odd effect, but we knew then that it was fair outside.'

Mr Frank says:
'It was about half past ten. I was upstairs in the Van Daan's part of the house, in Peter's room, doing schoolwork with him. Nothing could be heard. And if there really was anything to hear, I was at any rate not paying attention. I had just been giving Peter English dictation, and was saying to him: "Why, Peter, you know that *double* is spelled with only one *b* in English."'

Elli says:
'Mr Koophuis and Miep were writing and I was posting entries in the receipts book when a car drove up in front of the house. But cars often stopped, after all. Then the front door opened, and someone came up the stairs. I wondered who it could be. We often had callers. Only this time I could hear that there were several men. . . .'

Miep says:
'The footsteps moved along the corridor; then a door creaked, and a moment later the connecting door to Mr Kraler's office opened, and a fat man thrust his head in and said in Dutch: "Quiet. Stay in your seats."
'I started, and at first did not know . . . but then I knew.'

Mr Koophuis continues:
'I suppose I did not hear them because of the rumbling of the mills downstairs. The fat man's head was the first thing I saw, and then the door opened a little farther and I saw that there was another man standing in front of Kraler, asking him something. I think Kraler answered him. He was sitting at his desk, saying something, and then he rose slowly to his feet and went out with the man. I heard them on the stairs. There was nothing more he could do now.
'The fat man came in and planted himself in front of us. "You three stay here, understand?" he barked.
'So we stayed in the office and listened as someone else went upstairs, and doors rattled, and then there were footsteps everywhere. They searched the whole building.'

Mr Kraler wrote this account:
'It was a very fine summer day. Suddenly a staff sergeant of the "Green Police" and three Dutch civilians entered my office and asked me for the owner of the house. I gave them the name and address of our landlord. No, they said to me, we want the

person who is in charge here. That is myself, I replied. Then, ''Come along,'' they ordered.

'The police wanted to see the storerooms in the front part of the building, and I opened the doors for them. All will be well if they don't want to see anything else, I thought. But after the sergeant had looked at everything, he went out into the corridor, ordering me again to come along. At the end of the corridor they drew their revolvers all at once and the sergeant ordered me to push aside the bookcase at the head of the corridor and open the door behind it. I said: ''But there's only a bookcase there!'' At that he turned nasty, for he knew everything. He took hold of the bookcase and pulled at it; it yielded and the secret door was exposed. Perhaps the hooks had not been properly fastened. They opened the door, and I had to precede them up the steps. The policemen followed me; I could feel their pistols in my back. But since the steps were only wide enough for a single person, I was the first to enter the Franks' room. Mrs Frank was standing at the table. I made a great effort and managed to say: ''The Gestapo is here.''

'She did not start in fright, nor say anything in response.'

Otto Frank continues:

'I was pointing out to Peter his mistakes in the dictation when someone suddenly came running up the stairs. The steps creaked, and I started to my feet, for it was morning when everyone had to be quiet – but then the door flew open and a man stood before us holding his pistol aimed at my chest. The man wore civilian clothes.

'Peter and I raised our hands. The man told us to step forward, and we had to walk past him, and then he ordered us to go downstairs, while he followed us with the pistol.

'Downstairs all the others were already assembled. My wife and the children and the Van Daans were standing there with raised hands. Then Dussel came in, followed by another stranger. In the middle of the room stood a ''Green policeman''. He scrutinized our faces.'

The 'Green policeman' was accompanied by four or five Dutch Nazis. They wore plain-clothes and were 'eager beavers', behaving rather like the detectives in a movie thriller.

None of the occupants of the Secret Annexe had seriously counted on the possibility that they would be discovered. The terrors they had suffered at the beginning, the terrors of those first nights, which each had had to bear by himself, were by now largely faded. Only Mr Van Daan had continued to have occasional fits of despair; he had once hinted to Mr Frank that he could no longer endure life and that he would prefer the whole thing to be over, one way or another – he did not say precisely what he meant by this last phrase. But these crises were not due to premonitions of evil. He was worn out, while the others, the womenfolk, too, had become accustomed to the life they were leading.

In recent weeks, however, even Mr Van Daan had been in good spirits. The war was clearly approaching an end. Every news report made that clear, even the German Army communiques. The Russians were well into Poland; in Italy the Allies had reached Florence. American forces had broken through at Avranches, and the armies landed in Normandy were pouring with tremendous power into the heart of France. At the moment a solid German western front no longer existed, and it looked as though no new one would be formed until Holland was liberated. Twenty-five months had passed since Anne had made her diary entry describing their arrival at the house on the Prinsengracht. Fear cannot be maintained for twenty-five months. They were now full of confidence. Only two months before, Anne had written:

Perhaps, Margot says, I may yet be able to go back to school in September or October.

'And now they stood before us,' Mr Frank says. 'No, I had not imagined for so much as a moment what it would be like when they came. It was simply unthinkable. And now there they were.

'"Where is the storeroom?" they had asked downstairs. And now they asked: "Where are your valuables?"

'I pointed to the cupboard where my cashbox was kept. The "Green policeman" took it out. Then he looked around and reached for Anne's brief case. He shook everything out, dumped the contents on the floor, so that Anne's papers and notebooks and loose sheets lay scattered all over the floorboards. Then he put our valuables into the brief case, closed it, and asked us whether we had any weapons. But we had none, of course; anyway the plain-clothes men had already searched us thoroughly.

'Then he said: "Get ready. All of you be back here in five minutes."

'The Van Daans went upstairs to fetch their knapsacks; Anne and Dussel went into their room, adjoining ours, and I reached for my knapsack, which hung on the wall. Suddenly the Gestapo man stopped in front of my wife's bed, stared down at the chest that stood between bed and window, and exclaimed: "Where did you get this chest?"

'It was a grey foot-locker bound in iron, the kind we all had in the First War, and on the lid the words: "Reserve Lieutenant Otto Frank."

'"It is my own," I said.

'"How did you get it?"

'"I was an officer in the First War."

'The man became exceedingly confused. He stared at me, and finally said:

'"Then why didn't you report your status?"

'I bit my lips.

'"Why, man, you would have been treated decently! You would have been sent to Theresienstadt."

'I said nothing. Apparently he thought Theresienstadt a rest camp, so I said nothing. I merely looked at him. But he suddenly evaded my eyes, and all at once the perception came to me: Now he is standing at attention. Inwardly, this police sergeant has snapped to attention; if he dared, he might very well raise his hand to his cap in salute.

'Then he abruptly turned on his heel and raced upstairs. A moment later he came running down, and then he ran up again, and so he went, up and down, up and down, calling out: "Take your time!"

'He shouted these same words to us and to his agents.'

Mr Kraler writes:
'They were all utterly calm. They did not wail and lament. There was not much time for lamentations, for they had to pack their things, and so none of them betrayed their real feelings.'

Koophuis says:
'It all took a long time. The fat man had left the office, and we three were alone again. But we could not make an escape. The house is guarded, we thought. I considered: What was the first thing I had to do? And the next? And the thought kept running in my head: If only we hadn't involved the two girls.

'I said to Miep: "Try and get away. They may let you through. Go to my house and see whether you can help my wife and Corrie. They will certainly search my home."

'But Miep said she could not go now, that Henk had not come yet and now it was noon and he was sure to be along any moment. Then I tried the telephone. It was still working. I called my brother and told him what had happened, and he said at once: "I'll go over to your house."

'I hung up. Elli was standing at the window, crying and wringing her hands. You know, she was twenty-three, but at that moment she was nothing but a child. I left my desk, went over to her and said: "Here, take my brief case to the chemist on the corner. Tell him my brother will come and pick it up."'

Miep says:

'They must certainly have been in the building for at least an hour when one of the plain-clothes men came down, took a chair, and sat down in front of me, at my desk. He called some office and ordered a car to be sent over. "But a big one!" he added. "There are seven or eight of them." The voice on the telephone answered something, and the man said Yes and Good. Then he left us alone again.'

Mr Frank says:

'They gave us more time than we needed. We all knew what we had to pack – the same belongings we had planned on taking in case of fire.

'Once Anne came to me and I said: "No, don't take that, but you can take that along." And she obeyed, for she was very quiet and composed, only just as dispirited as all the rest of us. Perhaps that was why she did not think to take along one of her notebooks, which lay scattered about on the floor. But perhaps, too, she had a premonition that all was lost now, everything, and so she walked back and forth and did not even glance at her diary.

'No one wept. It was just that all of us were terribly dispirited. None of us said a word more than was absolutely necessary. In any case these policemen had distributed themselves among the rooms and watched us while we packed. The Gestapo man could still be heard on the steps. And at last the Van Daans came down. We were ready by then, too, and so we went out one after the other, through the open door. We left our hiding place, and went along the corridor and down the stairs. In the private office we had to wait again. Mr Kraler was already there when we came in and now Mr Koophuis entered, and one of the agents took up a position between the two of them. The "Green policeman" wanted to interrogate them, but both of them stated they had nothing to say to him. At that he exclaimed:

'"All right, then you'll come along too."'

Miep:

'And I heard them going, first in the corridor and then down the stairs; I could hear the heavy boots and the light footsteps, and then the very light footsteps of Anne. Through the years she had taught herself to walk so softly that you could hear her only if you knew what to listen for.

'I had seen her only the day before, and I was never to see her again, for the office door was closed as they all passed by.'

▷ Discuss the following:

1 What qualities of that morning does the writer give emphasis to?
2 How are sounds made dramatic in this piece?
3 What does the Gestapo reaction to the bookcase door tell us?
4 Why was the arrest such a surprise for the hiders at that particular time? How was this feeling expressed in Anne's Diary?
5 What was the Gestapo's first interest in the hiders? What effect did this interest have on the fate of the Diary?
6 What was ironic about the incident of Mr Frank's German officer's chest?
7 What was Anne's reaction to the arrest? Why do you think she abandoned the Diary?
8 What is particularly poignant about Miep's last report of Anne?

▷ Discuss in groups *or* list in writing the differences you notice between the two accounts in:
atmosphere, character, events, their portraits of Anne.

▷ Make a play scene out of the Ernst Schnabel version of the arrest.

▷ Imagine Anne continued writing her Diary after the arrest. Write her entry describing the events of Friday morning, 4 August 1944.

▷ Write Miep's description of the day of the arrest. If you can, compare your version with her account in her book *Anne Frank Remembered*.

A Czech Jewish girl photographed by the Gestapo. Anne might have looked like this after her arrest.

Auschwitz, in East Upper Silesia, Poland, was the most terrible of the Nazi concentration camps. Set up in 1940, it carried on its ghastly work until January, 1945. Two million of the six million Jews killed by the Nazis perished in its gas chambers and crematoria. Set on a main railway line that connected it easily with all parts of Europe, it grew to become a network of camps. Each 'transport', or trainload, of Jews was rapidly assessed at a 'selection' and divided up: those who were useless for war work – the old, the very young, women with children – went straight to the gas chambers; those fit for work in the factories of the locality survived, shaven, tattooed with numbers, dressed in coarse uniforms, herded into huts and compounds which were a sea of mud in winter, and full of choking dust in summer.

The girl who survived

Kitty Hart, a Jewish girl from Poland, was two years older than Anne Frank. She was sent to Auschwitz in 1942. By a mixture of luck, toughness and cunning, she survived and wrote vividly about her terrible experiences in *I am alive* (1961).

I was dozing, when the train suddenly halted. The doors of our cell swung open and we were driven out.
   'Austeigen, alles austeigen, schneller, los.'
   It was pitch dark, the middle of the night. We were ordered to stand in fives and be counted. I suddenly realized that there were hundreds of people. I could hear the sounds of whips, a lot of shouting and the barking of dogs. At last we were marched off. The ground felt muddy, and my feet stuck deep in the mire. Not far ahead were bright lights – a floodlit fence, and every few yards a guard was perched inside a small shelter up high on a pole. Then I saw an iron gate and written on it in large letters: Arbeit Macht Frei, *Work brings freedom.* This was Auschwitz I. But we passed by and carried on for some distance, walking along the railway tracks. On either side were fences and beyond – the unknown. At last we, the women only, passed through a gate. This was Auschwitz II – officially known as Birkenau, *Lager BIIa.*
   It was still rather dark, but we could make out in the distance queer looking figures streaming out of kind of huts. One could hear whistles and shouts of '*Aufstehen*', 'Get up'. '*Alles aufstehen zum Zahlappell*' – 'All stand for the count.' I wondered if I was hearing right. Was this really getting up time? It must have been three or four o'clock in the morning!
   We were led to a building known as the 'Sauna', apparently a Finnish word which meant 'baths'. Inside were showers and large drums where clothes were being deloused. I looked around. No German uniforms could be seen. Walking back and forth were some sort of creatures. Were they men or women? It was hard to tell. They had very short hair, some wore trousers, others kind of dresses. All had heavily painted red crosses on their backs. They did not talk but scream, and their voices were hoarse and deep, obviously from continuous shouting. Each had a whip in her

hand. I decided to have a closer look, and noticed on the left breast a number and a green triangle. As we were later to discover, a green triangle identified German prisoners, the criminal category. It was obvious what type of person ruled the camp and who held key positions there.

Someone dared ask, 'When do we get something to eat?' for we had nothing since leaving Dresden.

'Ha, so you are hungry already *Du verfluchtes Arschloch*?' came the barking reply. 'And what are you looking through the window for? Curious? Watching the *Muselmanns*? You will soon become a *Muselmann* yourself, don't you worry.'

Muselmann? What on earth does that mean? I could not make it out. This place seemed to have its own vocabulary, a complete language of its own. But I realized that we shall get acquainted with it before long. Soon we shall know everything.

A *Muselmann* was a living skeleton, and those figures in the distance looked just like skeletons. They walked slowly, dragging their feet, some even crawled along.

Someone plucked up courage and asked, 'Does one die here right away?'

'*Du blöde Kuh*,' came the reply. 'Look at me. I have been four years in here, do I look dead? Do you think you will be served with ham and eggs and have a nice warm bed waiting for you? You only die of a "cold".' She swung her whip over our heads, spat out and then turned away laughing to herself.

We were stripped and under showers for some time, and still there were no clothes. Next came the disinfection – a dip in a foul-smelling, bluish-green fluid. This over, the *Fryzerki*, the hairdressers, go to work. These were prisoners whose occupation was to shave our heads, under armpits and between our legs. The command was, 'Arms and legs out.' It only took a few seconds, I touched my head. It felt queer and cold.

Shaven-headed Jewish girls, 'selected' for camp work. Kitty and Anne would look like this.

I was thrown into a heap of rags – some clothing at last. There was a vest, a pair of khaki breeches and a blouse which had been part of a Russian prisoner of war uniform. The breeches were sizes too wide and too long, and the blouse had two odd sleeves. I had two odd stockings and a pair of wooden clogs, again sizes too big. I turned to look for Mother. I could not see her anywhere, in fact I could not recognize anyone at all.

In these clothes and with our heads shaved we all looked alike. When I finally did see her I just burst out laughing. Goodness, was that what I looked like too? We all looked like clowns out of a circus.

'*Anstellen, anstellen schneller, verfluchte Bande,*' cried a hoarse voice. It was time for the next procedure. At last it was my turn in the long line. It seemed first as though our particulars were being taken for I thought I could see pens and ink. The girls sitting at their desks looked respectable, and their hair seemed longer than any of the others we had seen so far. They were known as the *Schreibstube* – in camp language a sort of office worker, the camp elite. Theirs was an office job all right, but of an unusual sort. They were taking particulars of newcomers known as *Zugänge* and at the same time tattooing numbers on their arms. Mother was first, 39933, then I, 39934 below a triangle on my left forearm. There was a sharp pain each time the needle dug into the skin. I had never seen a tattoo before and it did not really worry me. I thought I could just wash it off when they had finished. I had not the faintest idea that it was a permanent mark.

The procedure took quite a few minutes and as the girl tattooed Mother's arm, she began to talk to her. Had we come straight from home? Home? We had forgotten what that meant a long time ago. She was amazed that Mother was allowed into the camp at all, for she informed us that all older people and small children were being segregated and taken over there – pointing through the window.

'And what is over there?' I asked.

'You will find that out soon enough,' she answered.

Kitty did find out when she was sent to work near the gas chambers and crematoria at Birkenau, one of the several camps that made up Auschwitz. Her job was a grim one: to sort out the belongings of the thousands of Jews exterminated by the Nazis.

As we marched along, we came to a small, but beautiful, wood full of birch trees. It was then that I understood the meaning of the word Birkenau or Brzezinki, for *Birke* in German means birch-tree, and the charming, wooded countryside was full of them. We admired the wonders of nature and had scarcely noticed that we were coming to the end of the little forest. Suddenly, there in front of us was the camp. The first thing that struck our eyes were some four very tall, wide, square chimneys and on coming closer, we saw peculiar low red brick buildings. As we walked through the gate I could recognize the sauna on the left. At the back of it was a well cultivated plot where vegetables were planted. Some distance behind that was a white house, surrounded by beautiful lawns and flower beds, giving the impression of a holiday resort. In actual fact, the white house was empty. Its inside walls were splashed with blood, the blood of innocent people, for in there death sentences by shooting were carried out. Often small transports of people were disposed of in this way.

Further inside the camp there was a proper road – the main Lagerstrasse. To the right, another narrower road, on each side of which stood two rows of well-built wooden huts, about six or seven to a row. Directly at the back of the huts were toilets, and then a wire fence. Immediately behind the fence was a wide, low red brick building with two very tall chimneys. This was Crematorium I. Directly behind it could be seen the outlines of Crematorium II. Over on the other side of the huts was another building of the same type. This was Crematorium III, and behind the sauna was Crematorium IV. And here we were in the very midst of it all – in hell on earth.

At the bottom, on the left-hand side, by the last huts, was a huge heap – it really looked like a mountain – as high at least as a three-story building. Piled up on the heap were goods of every description all jumbled up, suitcases, loose bundles of clothing, shoes, prams, food and even toys. These were the belongings of those already dead. Behind the heap was another fence, dividing our camp from that of the men.

Our huts were luxurious in comparison with those in the main camps. There were only about three hundred girls to a hut. Inside were three-tier single bunks, with well filled straw mattresses and two blankets each. There were even proper windows with a view – of the gas chambers and crematoria.

We had scarcely been inside a few minutes, than someone pulled me to the window. I did not want to look for I was too afraid of what I might see.

'You must see this, do you hear, you must,' said Isa with whom I palled-up on the way, and who was now one of our little family of four.

I raised my head and there not fifty yards away was a sight that staggered me. I had seen much, but never, never anything like this. I stood as if hypnotized. I could not move. I was actually witnessing with my very own eyes a murder, not of one person, but of hundreds of people, innocent people who had been led, mostly unsuspecting into a large hall. This was a sight that could *never* be forgotten. On the outside of the low building a ladder had been placed which reached up to a small opening. A figure in SS uniform climbed up briskly. At the top he pulled on a gas mask and gloves. Holding the opening with one hand, he pulled a bag out of his pocket, and swiftly threw the contents, a white powder, inside, shutting the opening immediately. In a flash he was down and, throwing the ladder on the lawn, ran away as if chased by a ghost.

At the same time the most terrifying screams echoed through the air, the desperate cries of suffocating people. I stood holding my breath, my hands pressed against my ears, but the cries were so loud, one would have thought the whole world must be able to hear them.

Someone shook me. 'It's over. Do you hear me, it's quiet. They are all dead now.'

It had taken about five to eight minutes.

Almost immediately a group of male prisoners approached from the men's camp. This was the *Sonderkommando* or *SD*, the very special *Kommando* which had to serve inside the crematoria. These men, there were about two to three hundred at a time, were usually caught for this kind of work within the camp. They were being replaced continually for most, after being there, either went insane or committed suicide. Often they were all killed, for it seemed that perhaps they knew just too much. They were the ones who had actually to burn the bodies. It often happened they burned their own parents, children or other relatives or friends.

I was still unable to take my eyes off one point. Everyone stared at one thing and now it happened. Smoke was beginning to billow out of the tall chimneys and soon sharp flames shot up six feet high into the sky. The black smoke became thicker and darker and choking, bringing with it a most peculiar smell, that of burning bodies, a smell of a singeing chicken would be comparable, but this stench of burnt fat and hair was unbearable. So what we had heard in the other camp really was true – the rumours were not exaggerated. Here were the death factories. As evening came, the whole sky was red, as if lit up. Smoke and flames poured out of all the chimneys which surrounded our little camp. It seemed as if blood was coming out, as indeed it was. No one slept that night, we just stood by the windows listening and watching.

The summer was beautiful. It was very hot and we on night shift found it difficult to sleep during the day. We were usually up early in the afternoon and on fine days we lay outside on the lovely lawn that surrounded our hut, sunbathing and splashing ourselves with water to cool off. We would dance and sing and even formed a little band. We began to laugh and joke again. In the evenings and Sunday afternoons the orchestra from the men's camp came over to play for us. Once we even staged a three-act play. I spent many hours reading the books that I had found while making up bundles. This was surely the craziest set-up in the whole world. All around us were screams, death, smoking chimneys making the air black and heavy with soot and the smell of burning bodies. I think our main fight was for sanity and so we laughed and sang with the burning hell all around us.

It was incredible, we lay sunbathing and not two yards away, divided only by a thin wire fence, columns of people of all nationalities were passing by on their way to the sauna and to the gas chambers. Often selections took place in the sauna, and these people were, in fact, lining up either to die or to be allowed to rot in the camps. Only young people were allowed into the camp – and then not always. All others passed by us to go to Crematorium III. It was strictly forbidden to communicate with these people, to tell them what really was here, and as there was usually a fair number of green uniforms around it was hardly ever possible. Most of them walked in unsuspecting. Only some looked uneasy. How could they imagine what was to come? Everything had been so cunningly disguised. They looked at us – we appeared well fed and well dressed, even sunbathing. It is true the queer building puzzled them and often they would ask us when passing, 'Do you girls work in those factories over there?' pointing to the crematoria.

Or they would ask, 'What is being made in those factories?' Occasionally the truth would dawn on them and then panic broke loose. But there were the dogs and the machine-guns, and soon the fighting was under control.

Passing us were women, poor and rich, tired looking, clutching their children and babies. Men were hanging on to their belongings and families. Sometimes a small child wheeled a doll in a little pram, or jumped over a skipping rope. A mother would change a baby's nappie while waiting, or put a bonnet over a child's head lest the sun would be too hot for it. A child would pick a flower which grew near the road. Nearby, SS man Wagner walked slowly looking very pleased with himself; he saw the child pick the flower and gave him a kick in passing.

All this time we just lay on the lawn and watched. It was quite unbelievable that this lovely baby, or this little boy playfully running backwards and forwards would be dead within the next few hours or minutes. Someone of our group gets up to look behind the block and then someone else shouts, 'You need not go and look. They are already burning, can't you smell?' Indeed the wind blows the smoke our way, causing us to cough and choke.

It was just a nightmare and it took weeks and weeks before I could really believe this was happening. The lovely children, the mother, the father all burning into ashes. I saw them walk, pass close by, go in, heard the screams, saw the fire, handled their belongings, and still I could not believe. But in the end I, like the rest of them, got used to it.

Kitty Hart: *I am alive*

A glimpse of Anne's life in Auschwitz

In his book, *The Footsteps of Anne Frank*, Ernst Schnabel traced some survivors who had known the Franks in Auschwitz. In the following extract, a woman who survived provides us with a few glimpses of what Anne's life was like there.

'On the third night the train suddenly came to a stop. The doors of the truck were slid violently open, and the first we saw of Auschwitz were the glaring searchlights fixed on the train, and outside on the platform men were running back and forth as though they were crazy to show how hard they were working. Those were the Kapos, whom we would soon get to know. Behind them, at the rear of the platform, stood the SS officers. They could be seen distinctly against the light. They were trimly built and smartly dressed, and had big dogs at their sides. As I watched, one of them stooped and patted his dog. The SS men who had accompanied our train went over to them. Now they wore their caps, which they had used to make collections from truck to truck, neatly at the prescribed angle on their heads.

'But all that was only a moment's glimpse, for now people began pouring out of the train, thronging the platform, and the Kapos shouted: "Faster, faster!" And then a loudspeaker drowned out all the voices, roaring:

'"Women to the left! Men to the right!"

'I saw them as they went away, Mr Van Daan and Mr Dussel and Peter and Mr Frank, all of them being driven to the right. But I saw no sign of my husband. He had suddenly vanished.

'"Listen!" the loud-speaker bawled again. "It is an hour's march to the women's camp. For children and the sick there are lorries waiting at the end of the platform."

'Selection' of Jews arriving at the 'ramp' in Auschwitz. SS soldiers and 'Kapos' in striped uniforms divide those who can work from those who will die at once in the gas chambers.

'We could see the lorries; they were painted with big red crosses. But we had no chance to reach them, we could see that at once, for everyone made a rush for them – and who among us was not sick and done in after those days on the train? Knots of people were still hanging on to them as they started off. No one had put a stop to the far too many who were crowding in. But the lorries did not go very far. Not one of those who went along on the lorries ever arrived at the women's camp, and no one ever found any trace of them.

'When we reached the Auschwitz-Birkenau women's camp, we were assigned to Block 29. That night march had been frightful. They had hustled us along at a brutal pace, but one woman helped the other, and so none fell behind. After we reached the barracks I could not help thinking: How is it that not a single one of us threw herself down on the ground and let herself be trampled to death or shot?

'I don't know whether I am using the term correctly, but I might say, for example, that Anne still had her face, up to the last. Actually she seemed to me in Auschwitz even more beautiful than in Westerbork, although she now no longer had her long hair. On our arrival our heads had been shaved; they needed women's hair – for power belting and pipe-joint packing in U-boats, I think. But now you could see that her beauty was wholly in her eyes, in her eyes alone, which seemed to grow bigger the thinner she became. Her gaiety had vanished, but she was still lively and sweet, and with her charm she sometimes secured things that the rest of us had long since given up hoping for.

'For example, we had no clothing apart from a grey sack, and under that we were naked. But when the weather turned cold, Anne came into the barracks one day wearing a suit of men's long underwear. She had begged it somewhere. She looked screamingly funny with those long white legs, but somehow still charming.

'We were divided into groups of five for roll-call, work, and distribution of food. You see, we had only one cup to each group of five. Anne was the youngest in her group, but nevertheless she was the leader of it. She also distributed the bread in the barracks, and she did it so well and fairly that there was none of the usual grumbling.

'Here is another example. We were always thirsty, so thirsty that at roll-call we would stick out our tongues if it happened to be raining or snowing, and many became sick from bad water. But the thirst was worse than any sickness. And once, when I was so far gone that I almost died because there was nothing to drink, Anne suddenly came to me with a cup of coffee. To this day I don't know where she got it.

'She, too, was the one who saw to the last what was going on all around us. We had long since stopped seeing. Who bothered to look when the flames shot up into the sky from the crematoria at night? Or when in the neighbouring barracks they suddenly ordered, ''Block closed'', and we knew that now people were being selected and gassed? It scarcely troubled us – we were beyond feelings. We scurried when the Kapos shouted their everlasting ''Faster, faster!'' We dug up sods of grass, twelve hours in succession, although the sods were no longer of any use because the Russians were coming closer day by day, and all we did was to toss the sods in a heap; but they drove us on and we dug out the sods and put up no resistance, not even in thought any more. *They* did not care how many died at work, and we scarcely cared either. The principal thing was that we brought the dead back, so that the count would be in order.

'We scarcely saw and heard these things any longer. Something protected us, kept us from seeing. But Anne had no such protection, to the last. I can still see her standing at the door and looking down the camp street as a herd of naked gypsy girls was driven by, to the crematorium, and Anne watched them going and cried. And she cried also when we marched past the Hungarian children who had already been waiting half a day in the rain in front of the gas chambers, because it was not yet their turn. And Anne nudged me and said: "Look, look. Their eyes . . .''

'She cried. And you cannot imagine how soon most of us came to the end of our tears.

'Later they gassed only the sick, the ones whose cases were quite hopeless, for the Russians were now so close that they might reach us in a single advance. Word went around the camp that the SS were beginning to hide the traces of what they had done. I began to hope again, for if the Russians came soon enough . . .

'Then Judy was taken away. It happened very fast. There was the sudden cry of "Block closed!" and we all had to undress and pass by an SS doctor, who picked out the youngest and strongest for a munitions factory in Czechoslovakia. Judy was one of the first taken, and Anne and Margot would certainly have gone also, and survived, except that they had scabies and the doctor rejected them.

'That was on October 27. On October 30 there was another "selection". The block was closed again, but this time we had to wait naked on the mustering ground, and it took a long time. Then we had to file singly, one behind the other, into the barracks, and inside a searchlight was set up. There stood the doctor, and we had to step into the light. By this time we saw that he picked out a great many who were not too sick or old, and then we knew that they would escape and that the old and sick would be gassed after all.

'In front of us stood a woman who was sixty, but she said she was forty and she was allowed to go along to Belsen.

'Then it was my turn, and I, too, made myself ten years younger. I called out to the doctor: "I am twenty-nine. And I have never had dysentery yet.''

'But he jerked his thumb and sent me to join the old and sick.

'Then came Mrs Frank – and she, too, joined our group at once.

'Then it was the turn of the two girls, Anne and Margot. Even under the glare of that searchlight Anne still had her face, and she encouraged Margot, and Margot walked erect into the light. There they stood for a moment, naked and shaven-headed, and Anne looked over at us with her unclouded face, looked straight and stood straight, and then they went on. We could not see what was on the other side of the searchlight. Mrs Frank screamed: "The children! Oh God . . .''

▷ Discuss the following:

1 What do you find most horrific and disturbing about the descriptions of Auschwitz by Kitty Hart?
2 What were the reasons for the selections on the railway platform at Auschwitz?
3 Why do you think there was so little protest among the Jews gathered in the camp?
4 What were the Nazis' intentions in their inhumane treatment: the loss of clothes, the shaving, the numbering?

▷ Write imaginatively about some of the people in the pictures on pages 37 and 41.

▷ Imagine that Anne continued her Diary while in Auschwitz. Using material from all the extracts, write some Diary entries to describe some parts of her life there.

The return of Mr Frank

Otto Frank was the only survivor among the hiders. By a mixture of good fortune (he was in Auschwitz hospital during the last weeks of the camp's operations) and physical and mental toughness (he had endured a soldier's life on the Western Front in the First World War), he stayed alive. After being taken from Poland to Odessa by the Russians, he travelled on a New Zealand ship to Marseilles in France, and from there made his way back to Holland.

He returned to his place in the business, Travies and Co. Deeply moved by his daughter's Diary, which had been preserved for him by Miep, he was persuaded to publish it. Thereafter he played an important part in the setting up of the Anne Frank Foundation, which preserved the Secret Annexe as a memorial and which is still dedicated to the fight against racial and religious intolerance.

After lodging for a time with Miep, Otto Frank was remarried to another Auschwitz survivor in 1953, and went to live near his old mother in Switzerland. He died in 1980.

Miep Gies tells the story of Otto's return to Amsterdam in June 1945.

Day after day Henk went to the Centraal Station and gave vouchers to returning Dutchmen, most of whom had lost everything and had either lost or been separated from their families. Day after day he would ask, 'Do you know Otto Frank? Have you seen the Frank family, Otto, Edith, Margot and Anne?' And day after day head after head would shake, 'No.' Or, 'No, I have not seen or heard of these people.'

Undaunted by this, Henk would ask the next person and the next, 'Do you know the Franks?' Always expecting one more ravaged head to shake, he finally heard a voice reply to his question, 'Mister, I have seen Otto Frank, and he is coming back!'

Henk flew home that day to tell me. It was 3 June 1945. He ran in the living-room and grabbed me, 'Miep, Otto Frank is coming back!'

My heart took flight. Deep down I'd always known that he would, that the others would too.

Just then my eye caught sight of a figure passing outside our window. My throat closed. I ran outside.

There was Mr Frank himself, walking toward our door.

We looked at each other. There were no words. He was thin, but he'd always been thin. He carried a little bundle. My eyes swam. My heart melted. Suddenly I was afraid to know more. I didn't want to know what had happened. I knew I would not ask.

We stood facing each other, speechless. Finally Frank spoke.

'Miep,' he said quietly. 'Miep, Edith is not coming back.'

My throat was pierced. I tried to hide my reaction to his thunderbolt. 'Come inside,' I insisted.

He went on, 'But I have great hope for Anne and Margot.'

'Yes. Great hope,' I echoed encouragingly. 'Come inside.'

He still stood there. 'Miep, I came here because you and Henk are the ones closest to me who are still here.'

I grabbed his bundle from his hand. 'Come, you stay right here with us. Now some food. You have a room here with us for as long as you want.'

He came inside. I made up a bedroom for him and put everything we had into a fine meal for him. We ate. Mr Frank told us that he'd come from Odessa to Marseilles by ship, and then by train and truck to Amsterdam. He had ended up in Auschwitz. That was the last time he'd seen Edith, Margot and Anne. The men had been separated from the women immediately. When the Russians liberated the camp in January, he had been taken on a very long trip to Odessa. Then from there to Marseilles and, at last, to Holland.

He told us these few things in his soft voice. He spoke very little, but between us there was no need for words.

Mr Frank settled in with Henk and myself. Right away he came back to the office and took his place again as the head of the business. I know he was relieved to have something to do each day. Meanwhile, he began exploring the network of information on Jews in the camps, the refugee agencies, the daily lists, the most crucial word-of-mouth information, trying everything to get news about Anne and Margot.

When Aushwitz had been liberated, Frank had gone right away to the women's camp to find out about his wife and children. Despite the chaos and desolation of the camps after the liberation, he had learned that Edith had died shortly before the liberation.

He had also learned that in all likelihood Anne and Margot had been transferred to another camp, along with Mrs Van Daan. The camp was called Bergen-Belsen and was quite a distance from Auschwitz. That was as far as his trail had gone so far, though. Now he was trying to pick up the search.

As far as the other men went, Frank had lost track of Dussel. He had no idea what had happened to him after the transit camp of Westerbork. Mr Van Daan he had seen with his own eyes on his way to be gassed. And Peter Van Daan had come to visit Frank when Frank was a patient in the Auschwitz infirmary. Frank knew that just before the liberation of the camp the Germans had taken groups of prisoners with them on their retreats. Peter had been in one of these groups.

Frank had begged Peter to try to get into the infirmary where Frank was, but Peter couldn't or wouldn't. He had last been seen going off with the retreating Germans into the snow-covered countryside. There was no further news about him.

Frank held high hopes for the girls because Bergen-Belsen was not a death camp. There were no gassings there. It was a work camp, filled with hunger and disease but with no apparatus for liquidation. Because Margot and Anne had been sent to the camp later than most other inmates they were relatively healthy. I, too, lived on hope for Anne and Margot. In some deep part of me, like a rock, I counted on their survival and their safe return to Amsterdam.

Mr Frank had written for news to several Dutch people who he had learned had been in Bergen-Belsen. Daily he waited for answers to his letters and for the new lists to be released and posted. Anne's sixteenth birthday was coming on 12 June. Perhaps, we hoped. But then the birthday came and went, and still no news.

One morning Mr Frank and I were alone in the office, opening the mail. Each of us had several pieces of mail. He was standing beside me, and I was sitting at my desk. I was vaguely aware of the sound of a letter being slit open. Then a moment of silence. Something made me look away from my mail. Then Frank's voice, flat, defeated, 'Miep.'

My eyes looked up at him, seeking out his eyes.

'Miep,' he gripped a sheet of paper in both his hands. 'I've got a letter from the nurse in Rotterdam. Miep, Anne and Margot are not coming back.'

We stayed there like that, both struck by lightning, burnt thoroughly through our hearts, our eyes fixed on each other. Then Mr Frank walked towards his office and said in that defeated voice, 'I'll be in my office.'

I heard him walk across the room and down the hall, and the door closed.

Dying girl, aged 17, sketched by the British war artist, Mervyn Peake, at Belsen concentration camp, 1945.

When Anne and Margot arrived in Belsen in late 1944, it was grossly overcrowded and full of typhus. Food supplies had virtually ceased, and the prisoners were left to rot in the decaying barracks. Both Margot and Anne died of typhus in February or March 1945. Belsen was liberated by the British Army in April.

I sat at my desk, utterly crushed. Everything that had happened before I could somehow accept. Like it or not, I had to accept it. But this I couldn't accept. It was the one thing I'd been sure would not happen.

I heard the others coming into the office. I heard a door opening and a voice chattering. Then good-morning greetings and coffee cups. I reached into the drawer on the side of my desk and took out the papers that had been waiting there for Anne for nearly a year now. No one, including me, had touched them. Now Anne was not coming back for her diary.

I took out all the papers, placing the little red-orange checked diary on top, and carried everything to Frank's office.

Frank was sitting at his desk, his eyes murky with shock. I held out the diary and the papers to him. I said, 'Here is your daughter Anne's legacy to you.'

I could tell that he recognized the diary. He had given it to her just over three years before on her thirteenth birthday, just before going into hiding. He touched it with the tip of his fingers. I pressed everything into his hands, then I left his office, closing the door quietly.

Shortly afterwards the phone on my desk rang. It was Mr Frank's voice. 'Miep, please see to it that I'm not disturbed,' he said.

'I've already done that,' I replied.

Miep Gies: *Anne Frank Remembered*

▷ Using Miep's memoir, write the story of Otto's return from his point of view. End as he begins to read the Diary.

▷ Make two play scenes out of Miep's memoir:

1 Otto's return: beginning with Henk's news from the station,
2 from receiving the letter about Anne to the opening of the Diary.

Poems about the Holocaust

During the war, Primo Levi, the great Jewish-Italian writer, was a partisan, fighting the Fascists in German-occupied northern Italy. In December 1943, he was captured and taken to the transit camp at Fossoli. In February 1944, the prisoners heard that they were to be taken to Auschwitz. They knew that this meant death. In fact only 24 of the 640 'pieces', as they were called, survived.

Levi felt keenly his responsibility as a surviving witness and was determined that the Nazi slaughter of the Jews would not be forgotten. 'Shema' (Hear!) is a great Jewish prayer, chanted especially by martyrs in Hebrew history. Some of the six million who died in the camps were heard to say it as they went to execution.

Shema

You who live secure
In your warm houses,
Who, returning at evening, find
Hot food and friendly faces:
  Consider whether this is a man,
  Who labours in the mud
  Who knows no peace
  Who fights for a crust of bread
  Who dies at a yes or a no.
  Consider whether this is a woman,
  Without hair or name
  With no more strength to remember
  Eyes empty and womb cold
  As a frog in winter.
Consider that this has been:
I command these words to you.
Engrave them on your hearts
When you are in your house, when you walk on your
  way
When you go to bed, when you rise:
Repeat them to your children.
  Or may your house crumble,
  Disease render you powerless,
  Your offspring avert their faces from you.

Primo Levi

▷ Who are the man and woman described here? Which descriptive detail of them do you find most frightening? What is Levi afraid of in this poem?

The Polish poet, Tadeusz Rosewicz, visiting the grim museum set up at Auschwitz after the war, was impressed by the mounds of human hair cut from prisoners, supposedly for use in German war industry.

Pigtail

When all the women in the transport
had their heads shaved
four workmen with brooms made of birch twigs
swept up
and gathered up the hair

Behind clean glass
the stiff hair lies
of those suffocated in gas chambers
there are pins and side combs
in this hair

The hair is not shot through with light
is not parted by the breeze
is not touched by any hand
or rain or lips

In huge chests
clouds of dry hair
of those suffocated
and a faded plait
a pigtail with a ribbon
pulled at school
by naughty boys.

Tadeusz Rozewicz, Trans. Adam Czerniawski

▷ Which details of the hair are peculiarly horrific in verses two and three? Why is the pigtail with the ribbon mentioned particularly? What does the hair represent about the people it once belonged to?

For your coursework folder

▷ Write about these poems for the poetry section of your GCSE folder. Find other poems about the Holocaust and include them in your folder. Say what the poems are about and state which impressed you most. Give careful reasons for your opinions and illustrate your answers with brief quotations.

Work suggestions using the whole text

▷ Anne writes one of her essays, describing the other hiders and helpers.

▷ Margot also wrote a diary, which was lost. Compose some of her entries about some key episodes of the time in hiding – about Anne's relationship with Peter, for example.

▷ Write imaginatively about some of Mr Frank's worries and concerns in the Annexe.

▷ A journalist visits the Annexe in 1947, after the first publication of the Diary. Write his story for the newspaper. Include some brief interviews and some striking headlines.

▷ Choose one or two moments of a) comedy, and b) terror, as recorded in the Diary. Describe what happens in them in your own words.

▷ Use the school library to compile a short, illustrated study project of the concentration camps (especially those connected with Anne) and Hitler's 'Final Solution'.

▷ Imagine Peter's view of Annexe life and people, concentrating on a few incidents.

▷ Look up some of the books noted in the Further Reading section of the Longman Imprint edition of *The Diary of Anne Frank*, especially:

Primo Levi: *If this is a man*,
Hans Richter: *Friedrich*,
Kitty Hart: *I am alive*,
Art Spiegelman: *Maus*.

Read and review one or more of the books.

▷ Compare the Diary with the play version (Blackie Student Drama series). Concentrate on events, characters and the portrait of Anne.

▷ Write a general review of the Diary, aiming it at other readers of your age. Here is a possible plan:

1 introduction: the facts about the Diary and its publication,
2 brief outline of the events it describes,
3 description of the hiders and the helpers,
4 particular episodes that impressed you,
5 qualities of Anne and her writing that interested you,
6 summing up: why people should read the Diary and why it is important.

THE DIARY OF
LONGMAN
IMPRINT BOOKS
ANNE FRANK

Longman Imprint Books

The Diary of Anne Frank

ISBN 0 582 01736 X

This edition of the Diary has been specially prepared by Christopher Martin. As well as background notes explaining the Nazi persecution of the Jews, there are photographs of the Frank family and the secret Annexe, and source material on the concentration camps. Substantial reading and further information lists are included.